Little
Pebble™

Staying
Safe

Stranger
Safety

by Sarah L. Schuette

PEBBLE
a capstone imprint

Little Pebble is published by Pebble
1710 Roe Crest Drive
North Mankato, Minnesota 56003
www.mycapstone.com

Library of Congress Cataloging-in-Publication Data
Names: Schuette, Sarah L., 1976– author.
Title: Stranger safety / by Sarah L. Schuette.
Description: North Mankato, Minnesota : Pebble,
[2020] | Series: Little pebble. staying safe! | Audience:
Age: 6–8. | Audience: K to Grade 3. | Includes
bibliographical references and index. Identifiers: LCCN
2018052508| ISBN 9781977108708 (hardcover) | ISBN
9781977110336 (pbk.) | ISBN 9781977108784 (ebook
pdf) Subjects: LCSH: Children and strangers—Juvenile
literature. | Safety education—Juvenile literature. | Crime
prevention—Juvenile literature. Classification: LCC
HQ784.S8 S38 2019 | DDC 613.6071—dc23
LC record available at https://lccn.loc.gov/2018052508

Editorial Credits
Erika L. Shores, editor; Heidi Thompson, designer;
Morgan Walters, media researcher; Marcy Morin,
scheduler; Tori Abraham, production specialist

Photo Credits
All photos by Capstone Studio/Karon Dubke

All internet sites appearing in back matter were available
and accurate when this book was sent to press.

The author dedicates this book to her mother, Jane
Schuette, who always made sure to use their safe word.

Capstone thanks Shonette Doggett, coalition
coordinator, Safe Kids Greater East Metro/St. Croix
Valley, St. Paul, Minnesota, for reviewing this book.

Printed and bound in China.
001671

Table of Contents

Who Is a Stranger?

A stranger is a person

you don't know.

How to Be Safe

Stay close!

Play where a trusted adult

can see you.

Stay together!

Kate and Erin play

in a group.

Tyler never goes with people he doesn't know. He asks his dad first.

A person gives Meg
a bad feeling.
She stays away.

Lin thinks about
her feelings.

She writes them down.

Tell!

Sam won't keep secrets.

It's not OK for anyone

to hurt him.

Run! Yell!

A person tries to grab him.

Nico knows to get away.

People Help

Not all strangers are bad.

Many people are helpful.

Glossary

feeling—an emotion such as sadness, fear, joy, or worry

secret—information only known to a few people; adults should never ask children to keep secrets

stranger—a person you do not know; even if a stranger knows your name, they might not be a safe person

trusted adult—a grown-up who is truthful

Read More

Greenwood, Nancy. *Be Aware of Stranger Danger.* Keep Yourself Safe on the Internet. New York: PowerKids Press, 2018.

Hicks, Dwayne. *Rules in the Playground*. Rules at School. New York: PowerKids Press, 2020.

Kallio, Jamie. *12 Tips for Staying Safe*. Healthy Living. Mankato, MN: 12-Story Library, 2017.

Internet Sites

Kid Smartz Videos
www.kidsmartz.org/Videos

Safety4Kids
www.safety4kids.com.au/safety-zone_stranger-danger

Super-cool stuff!

Check out projects, games, and lots more at
www.capstonekids.com

Critical Thinking Questions

1. What should you do if someone tries to grab you?

2. Why is it safer to play in a group than by yourself?

3. Community helpers are people whose jobs it is to help others. Can you name some helpers in your city or town?

Index